COWGIRL

by Murray Tinkelman

Greenwillow Books, New York

Barrel racing is the cowgirl's event. The racer may take a running start into the arena as she begins riding a cloverleaf pattern around three brightly colored barrels. The rider races for the first barrel, reins her horse sharply around it, and makes for the second barrel, another tight turn and she heads for the last barrel at the far end of the arena. After the final barrel turn is made, she spurs her horse for the full-speed race back to the finish line. Electronic timers record the barrel racer's time from start to finish. A five-second penalty is added for any barrel tipped over during an event. Under seventeen seconds is considered excellent time for a completed course. ★ From *Rodeo* by Murray Tinkelman

☆ TO TRACY PEARSON—A CHAMPION ☆

LIBRARY OF CONGRESS CATALOGING IN PUBLICATION DATA

TINKELMAN, MURRAY. COWGIRL

SUMMARY: A YOUNG COWGIRL PARTICIPATES IN HER FIRST RODEO.
[1. COWGIRLS—FICTION. 2. RODEOS—FICTION] I. TITLE. PZ7.T489Co 1984
[E] 83-20581 ISBN 0-688-02882-9 ISBN 0-688-02883-7 (LIB. BDG.)

7.99

Tonight is the first time I will race my horse at a rodeo. We have been practicing all year.

I bathe and groom Lady and clean my equipment.
I always want my saddle and my horse clean.

I am too nervous to eat. I put my tack and saddle in the trailer and then load Lady onto the trailer.

I dress in my best western clothes. I am wearing brand-new boots and my good luck spurs. My mother will drive me to the rodeo.

We pull into the parking field. I unload Lady and tie her to the side of the trailer so she can be fed and saddled.

I go to the rodeo office to pay my entry fee.
They give me a number that my mother pins to
my pant leg. I meet some cowgirl friends of mine.
A champion barrel racer wishes me good luck.

I ride in the grand entry. I try to stay calm so I won't make Lady nervous. It is so exciting. The band plays "The Star-Spangled Banner" and the rodeo begins.

I talk to the other cowgirls while waiting for the barrel racing to start. I will be the first barrel racer to run the course. I will set the pace.

The rodeo announcer calls my name over the public address system. I ride my horse to the starting line. I think of how I made this run in practice one hundred times.

I touch the spurs to Lady and we are off and running for the first barrel. Lady is running well, but when we turn the first barrel, my hat starts to slip over my eyes. I shove the hat back into place and keep going.

We take the turn at the second barrel a little too tightly and almost tip it over. If it fell, it would be a five-second penalty.

We circle the last barrel and race for the finish line. We slide to a stop and the crowd cheers. The announcer calls out the official time. We ran the barrels in 17.9 seconds. We did it— just like in practice.

The other cowgirls must do better to beat me. One does, her time is 17.0 seconds. But I finished second and I have won a beautiful silver buckle. I have done much better than I expected to. The other cowgirls congratulate me. I show them my trophy buckle.

I unsaddle Lady and walk her until she cools off. I let her drink a little water and I give her some carrots as a treat.

I load Lady and my equipment onto the trailer and Mom drives us home. I can hardly wait to tell my friends at the barn. I can hardly wait for the next rodeo. Maybe I will come in first. Maybe I can be a champion.